MW00666768

Concert and Contest COLLECTION

Compiled and Edited
by H. VOXMAN

for

B♭ TENOR SAXOPHONE with piano accompaniment

CONTENTS

		Page Numbers Solo Part	Piano Part
ADAGIO AND ALLEGRO *from Sonata No. 6*	G. F. Handel	22	52
ALLEGRETTO	A. Arensky	5	6
CONTRADANCE	W. A. Mozart	3	2
FIRST CONCERTINO	Georges Guilhaud	19	44
GIGUE *from Partita III*	J. S. Bach	24	Unaccompanied
MENUETTO AND PRESTO *from Trio V*	F. J. Haydn	7	10
NOVELETTE	Georges Sporck	18	41
OLD CASTLE, THE *from Pictures at an Exhibition*	M. Mussorgsky	10	20
PIECE IN G MINOR Op. 5	Gabriel Pierne	12	25
PRELUDE AND ALLEGRO	Leroy Ostransky	16	36
PREMIERE ETUDE DE CONCOURS	A. S. Petit	14	30
SINFONIA *(Arioso) from Cantata No. 156*	J. S. Bach	4	4
TWO LITTLE TALES	E. Desportes	8	14
VALSE NOUVELLE *from Album for the Young*	P. Tchaikovsky	6	8

RUBANK®

HAL•LEONARD® CORPORATION
7777 W. BLUEMOUND RD. P.O. BOX 13819 MILWAUKEE, WI 53213

COLLECTIONS IN THIS SERIES:

C Flute and Piano

B♭ Clarinet and Piano

B♭ Bass Clarinet and Piano

Oboe and Piano

Bassoon and Piano

E♭ Alto Saxophone and Piano

B♭ Tenor Saxophone and Piano

B♭ Cornet, Trumpet
or Baritone and Piano
(Baritone In Bass or Treble Clef)

French Horn (In F) and Piano

Trombone (Bass Clef) and Piano

E♭ or BB♭ Bass
(Tuba - Sousaphone) and Piano

Viola and Piano

Individually Compiled and Edited, Each Of the Collections Includes A Diversified Repertoire
The Solo Parts and Piano Accompaniments Are Published As Separate Books With A Durable Cover

Contradance

B♭ Tenor Saxophone

W. A. MOZART
Transcribed by H. Voxman

Sinfonia

(Arioso)

from Cantata No. 156*

Bb Tenor Saxophone

J. S. BACH

Transcribed by H. Voxman

* This Cantata was composed by Bach ca. 1730. The original scoring of the Sinfonia is for solo oboe, strings, and continuo. The eighth-note accompaniment figures (treble) should probably be played quasi pizzicato. Bach also used this melody in a more elaborate version in his F minor Concerto for Clavier.

Allegretto

B♭ Tenor Saxophone

A. ARENSKY
Transcribed by H. Voxman

Valse Nouvelle

from Album for the Young

B♭ Tenor Saxophone

P. TCHAIKOVSKY, Op. 39, No. 8
Transcribed by H. Voxman

Menuetto and Presto

from Trio V

B♭ Tenor Saxophone

F. J. HAYDN
Transcribed by H. Voxman

Two Little Tales

B♭ Tenor Saxophone

E. DESPORTES
Transcribed by H. Voxman

I - SENTIMENTAL

II - GAY

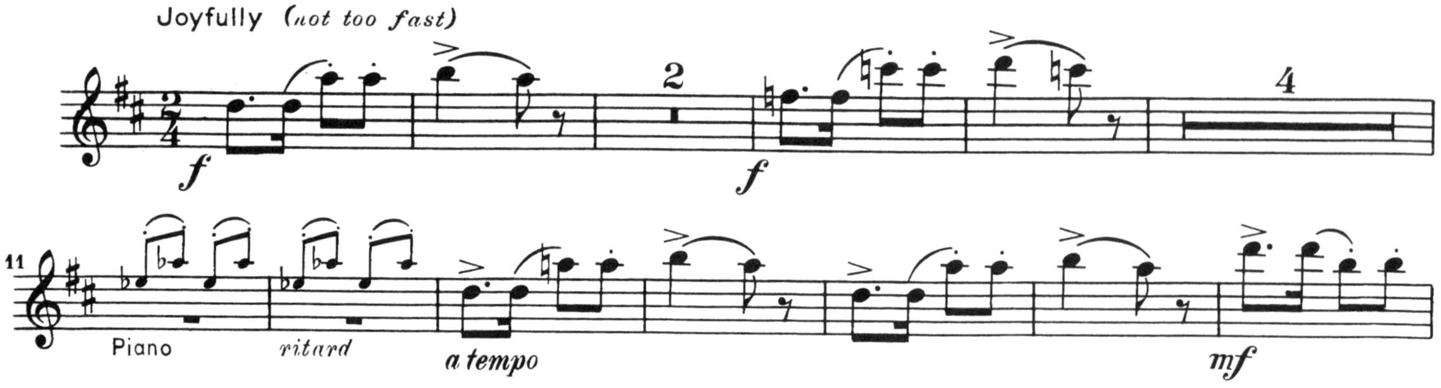

Tempo I
Lively
mf
f
poco rit.
f a tempo
ff
ritard

The Old Castle

from Pictures at an Exhibition

B♭ Tenor Saxophone

M. MUSSORGSKY
Transcribed by H. Voxman

47
p
55
cresc.
f
p
62
p
69
75
f
pp
81
1
88
pp
1
1
95
pp
espressivo
(9)
100
1
p
1
f

Pièce in G Minor

B♭ Tenor Saxophone

GABRIEL PIERNÉ, Op. 5
Transcribed by H. Voxman

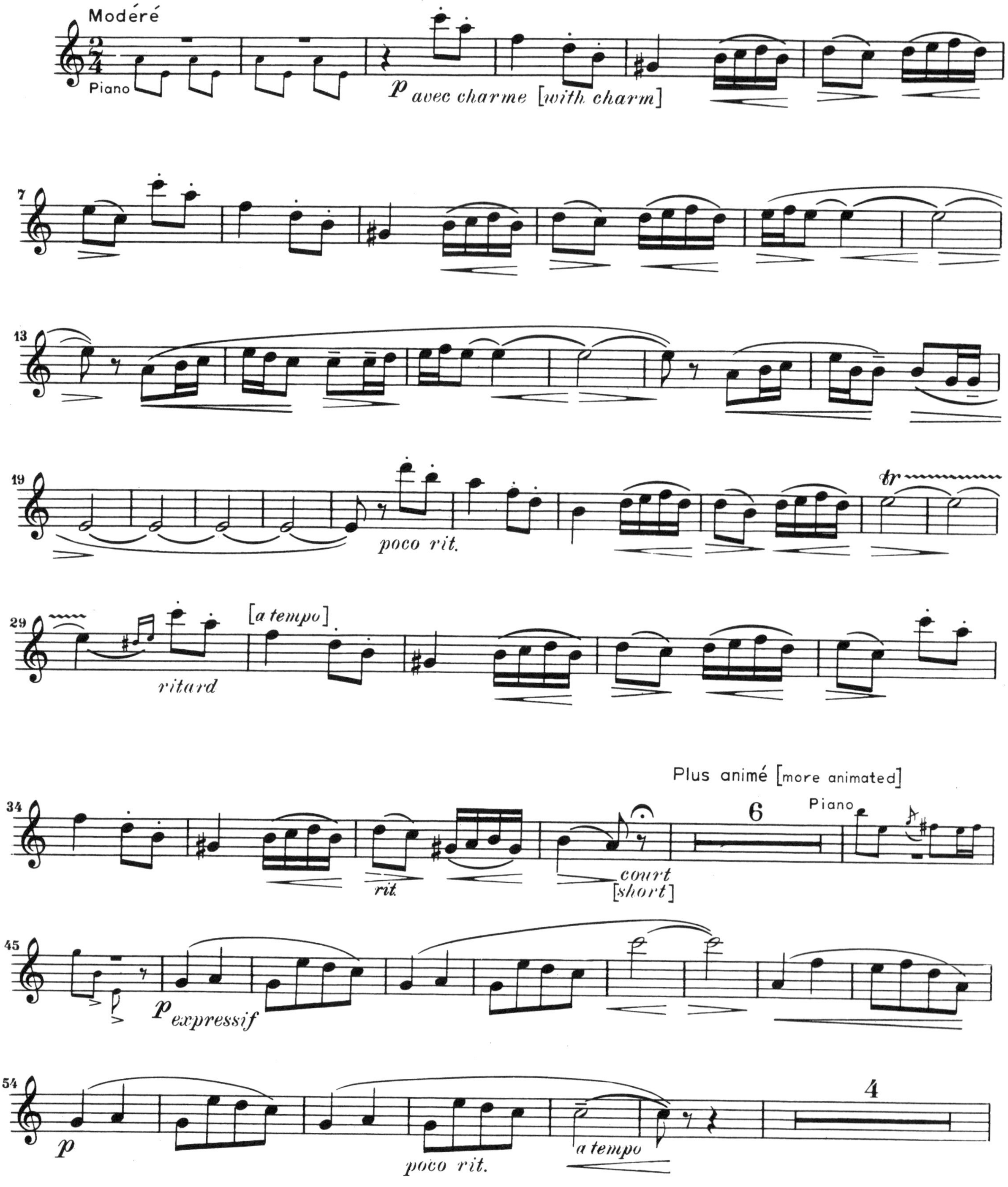

Piano
p
p subito
rit.
Tempo I
p
riten.

Première Étude de Concours

B♭ Tenor Saxophone

A. S. PETIT
Edited by H. Voxman

Polonaise (♩= 84)
6
poco rit.
dolce
p a tempo
Piano
p a tempo
Animato
Long
très décidé

Prelude and Allegro

Bb Tenor Saxophone

LEROY OSTRANSKY

(♩. = 69) In one
mp
mf
f
rit
a tempo
ff
poco meno mosso
Molto cantabile
p
accel.
Tempo I

Novelette

B♭ Tenor Saxophone

GEORGES SPORCK
Edited by H. Voxman

Lent (♩ = 50 *environ*)
avec beaucoup de laisser aller dans la mesure [*rather freely*]

First Concertino

B♭ Tenor Saxophone

GEORGES GUILHAUD
Transcribed by H. Voxman

Andante
cresc.
lunga
rit.
a tempo
rit.
rall.
a tempo
rall.
a tempo
a piacere
Allegro non troppo
Allegretto
cresc.

121
(rit.)
(a tempo)
mf
126
p
mf
p
rit.
130
f a tempo
136
p
cresc.
140
f
ff
4
mf cantabile
149
pp
cresc.
f
158
2
p
164
cresc.
f
lunga
a tempo
pp cantabile
169
cresc.
f
p
174
cres - - cen - - do
ff
178
allarg.
ff

Adagio and Allegro

(from Sonata No. 6 for Violin & Keyboard)

B♭ Tenor Saxophone

G. F. HANDEL
Transcribed by H. Voxman

cresc.
cresc.
cresc.
poco rit. on repeat

Gigue

from Partita III for Solo Violin

B♭ Tenor Saxophone
(Unaccompanied)

J. S. BACH
Transcribed by H. Voxman